*May God b[less you]
and home [...]*

Karmen Bernacchi

Still Waiting

BY

KARMEN BERNACCHI

Permissions:

"Believe Me Now" words and music by James Isaac Elliot and Steven Curtis Chapman© 2004 Sparrow Song (BMI) (Admin by CMG Capitol), Primary Wave Brian (Chapman SP Acct) (CMG Capitol) and Cabinetmaker Music (ASCAP) Sparrow Song Admin by CMG Capitol, Cabinetmaker Music Admin by ICG. All rights reserved. Used by Permission.

"What Now" words and music by Steven Curtis Chapman. © 2004 Sparrow Song (BMI) (Admin by EMI CMG Publishing) / Primary Wave Brian (Chapman Sp Acct) (BMI) All rights reserved. Used by permission.

"The Great Adventure" words and music by Geoff Moore and Steven Curtis Chapman. © 1992 Sparrow Song, Peach Hill Songs and Songs of the Forefront. Admin by CMG Capitol. All rights reserved. Used by permission.

"Joy in the Journey" words and music by Michael Card. © Warner/Chappell Music, Inc. Peermusic Publishing, Admin by CMG Capitol. All rights reserved. Used by permission.

"Welcome to Holland" © 1987 by Emily Perl Kingsley. All rights reserved. Used by permission of the author.

Scripture taken from the Holy Bible, NEW INTERNATIONAL VERSION®, NIV® Copyright © 1973, 1978, 1984, 2011 by Biblica, Inc.® Used by permission. All rights reserved worldwide.

Scripture also taken from the Holy Bible, King James Version, public domain.

Copyright © 2016 Karmen Bernacchi

All rights reserved.

ISBN-13: 978-1540336088
ISBN-10: 1540336085

DEDICATION

This book is dedicated to my daughter, Ella Joy SiHan. I waited for you. I prayed for you. I have loved you since the day God gave me the dream of you. Whatever lies ahead, whatever challenges you may face, always know that God had a plan and a purpose for you from the start. You were no accident. He made no mistake. You were His perfect creation. I hope you always know just how much you are loved. This is the story of our journey to you. It wasn't an easy road, but I wouldn't change a thing. I love you!

KARMEN BERNACCHI

CONTENTS

1	The Waiting Room	7
2	The Dream	11
3	Oh to be Doris Day!	17
4	The Shadow of Death	21
5	Lost in the Dark	27
6	I Surrender	37
7	Believe Me Now	43
8	Blazing the Paper Trail to our Daughter	49
9	Basket Weaving	53
10	Enough!	59
11	Love Never Gives Up	63
12	Fighting for Life	67
13	Time to Come Home!	75
14	A New Normal	89
15	A Complicated Diagnosis	93
16	A Matter of the Heart	103
17	Still Waiting	107
	Photo Album	113
	Acknowledgements	123

KARMEN BERNACCHI

1 - THE WAITING ROOM

*In the morning, O LORD, you hear my voice;
in the morning I lay my requests before you
and wait in expectation. – Psalms 5:3 (NIV)*

It almost seemed like a cruel joke. There I sat in this busy clinic waiting room, waiting for the results of a test that would inevitably make me feel like the emptiest, most defective woman on the planet. They had to take a pregnancy test before they could undergo any further procedures, but I knew in my heart it would be just like the dozens of tests I'd taken before … a big, fat minus sign. Negative. No baby for you!

As I sat in that waiting room, I couldn't help but feel like I'd spent my whole life in a waiting room of some type. Not all of them were waiting rooms like this one … sterile floors, three-year old magazines, quiet whispers from patients nervously waiting to take their turn … but it was a waiting room none the less. It was a big empty place, where I felt alone, helpless and forgotten. "God's

Waiting Room" – that's what I call it – and it's a room I knew all too well.

When I was a little girl my family moved a lot. It seemed I would just get settled in a new school and make new friends, and we were off and running again. My Dad always said he had "itchy feet", and he just had to keep moving. The truth was, no matter what state he was in, he could never seem to find real contentment.

My Dad went from being a Pastor to a fruit truck driver to a Pastor again to a mail carrier to a farmer to a Pastor again to a truck driver ... and it went on and on and on. Whatever job he had, it never made him feel complete.

My Dad was never truly happy. He always longed for something else ... something more than what he had. Whether it was in his career, his relationships or his possessions ... he always felt there had to be something more. His lack of contentment was hard on our family, and it was even harder on him. I don't think my Dad ever really realized how much he had in his life.

I lived under the shadow of my Dad's quest for something more, and as much as I loved him, I determined that I would not be like him. I saw the emptiness his discontentment wrought. I had resolved that I would have a more settled life.

Of course the "settled" life that I pictured included a beautiful lake-front home complete with a husband who adored me, three or four children, a dog, a swimming pool, a boat and a successful singing career. The only part of that picture that had come true was the adoring husband and the dog.

While I longed for my marriage to be enough, the truth was it wasn't. I could do without the lake-front home. I could live without the boat and the swimming pool. I didn't need a successful career as a musician – as long as I had an outlet for my music. I had Greg and I felt extremely blessed to have him in my life. Unfortunately the fulfillment I felt in my marriage only accentuated the emptiness I felt in our home. We wanted children, and I couldn't produce them – and that made me feel worthless as a woman.

Finally the nurse called my name, my heart leapt for a minute. What if this time was actually different? What if the test had come back positive? What if I could know what it was like to go home and tell my husband, "You are going to be a father!" My mind raced at the possibilities as I followed her down what seemed like an endless corridor.

As we walked into the cold room, I didn't need her to give me an answer. The x-ray equipment gave it away. The test was negative. None of the fertility drugs had worked. I still had not produced a child. I was defective and worthless. I felt like it was stamped across my forehead. As I sat on that cold metal table, waiting for yet another battery of tests to be done, the tears formed in my eyes. I already knew in my head what the test results would show, the final verdict was more than my heart could take and the tears began to flow.

I could hardly wait to get out of that room and race home where I could fall apart in private. I had undergone my last fertility treatment. There was nothing further the doctors could do for me without a very expensive procedure that we simply could not afford. Our journey to become parents appeared to be ending, but my journey to contentment and completeness as a woman most certainly was not. In fact, my journey was just beginning.

2 - THE DREAM

"For I know the plans I have for you," declares the LORD, "plans to prosper you and not to harm you, plans to give you hope and a future." – Jeremiah 29:11 (NIV)

Being a wife and mother wasn't always a priority for me. After high school I struck out on my own. I went to college for a year, then dropped out to pursue a career on the stage. My dreams of stardom didn't exactly pan out. In fact my dreams ran head-first into a brick wall of reality. Breaking into the entertainment industry was not as easy as I thought it would be, and so with few skills and no money, I moved back to my small home-town and tried to find my life.

By this time most of my friends were getting married and starting their families. I thought they were crazy. I had a theme song that went, "I don't wanna get married, I'm having too much fun. I don't wanna get tangled up with anyone. I have so many boyfriends to me they're all the same. To marry one and leave the rest would be a dirty shame."

I didn't really have a lot of boyfriends. To be honest, a relationship just didn't interest me. My sole focus was on music, acting and God. I wanted to use the gifts God had given me to make a difference in the world.

I wanted to see the world. I wanted to go on missions trips and help people. I had so many dreams and the last thing I wanted in my life was a man to complicate things. Then came Greg…

I was performing with a local community theatre group when I met him. At first we were just good friends. We loved performing together. He was (and still is) an excellent actor, and sharing the stage with him was a real pleasure. Our friendship continued to grow, but a dating relationship didn't start until several years later.

The summer of 1993, Greg invited me to a Barry Manilow concert in Milwaukee. A huge Barry Manilow fan, that was all it took. He had me wrapped around his little finger and we began dating. The strong friendship we had built over the years had built an excellent foundation for our relationship. We fell madly in love and were ready to start our future together.

Like any happy couple we immediately began dreaming of our future. Because we were getting married a little later than most (Greg was 32, I was 30) we wanted to start our family immediately. We had it all worked out. We would conceive on our honeymoon and start our family nine months later. Then about a year later we'd have number two and we'd continue on from there. Oh how naïve we were!

Three weeks after our wedding my brother Kurt married his beautiful wife Seleena in Las Vegas. Before the end of the year they announced that they were expecting their first child together. Yes, they got pregnant on their honeymoon. While I was happy for them, I was very disappointed for us because our plan was not working out like expected. It had been three months and still no baby. Was something wrong?

We didn't let it worry us too much at first. We spent the next year just enjoying being married, and working on that starting a family thing. After a year of trying to conceive we decided to get our doctors involved.

We saw a specialist and after a battery of tests it was determined that there was no real physical reason that we couldn't have a baby. They told us to relax, "enjoy the process" and come back next year if we still hadn't conceived.

Soon we were celebrating our second anniversary and still there was no baby in sight. My brother and his wife had given birth to an amazing little boy named Tyler. And had already made the announcement that they were pregnant again … with twins!

Our happiness for them was clouded by our own disappointment. The "twin" factor only served to accentuate our empty nest. Still I pasted on my best happy face and threw another baby shower for my sister-in-law, while my heart ached with a longing for a child of our own.

After the birth of the twins, Jacob and Jonathan, we began more aggressively pursuing our infertility issues. The doctor started me on Clomid and warned me about the possibilities of multiple birth with its use.

Yes! Multiple birth sounded just perfect to us! The more the merrier! We were thrilled to begin this new regimen and felt certain that we were finally on the path to starting our family. Unfortunately, our excitement would soon give way to more frustration as month after month we would continue to be disappointed.

My doctor increased my dosage of Clomid and we felt certain that would do the trick. But after several more months at that level we still hadn't conceived. So the doctor increased my dosage to the maximum amount. A few more months passed and still nothing.

Because Clomid wasn't covered by our insurance, we knew we couldn't continue the regimen indefinitely. It was an expensive drug and it was obviously unsuccessful in helping us conceive.

The doctor recommended another drug to us but it was very expensive. At a cost of about $1,500 per month, we knew we couldn't use it for long. Our doctor noted that we could obtain the drug from Canada or Mexico at a significantly reduced price. He suggested perhaps we should take a trip to one of these countries and stock up on the medication.

We considered his advice and thought long and hard about it. But felt in our heart of hearts that this was not the right course for us. Instead we sought a second opinion at a fertility clinic in a nearby city. The results were the same. Nobody was saying we couldn't have children. We just couldn't seem to make it happen.

My new doctor recommended we try in vitro fertilization. They told us the cost was approximately $15,000 and our chances of conception would be approximately one in three. We told them we would need some time to consider their recommendations, but went home knowing in our hearts that our medical road to conception had officially ended.

We didn't have $15,000. Our insurance wouldn't cover any of the procedure. We hadn't given up on having a biological child, but we were beginning to realize that if it was going to happen it would take a miracle.

We had been praying for a miracle all along, but we were just beginning to realize how totally dependent on God we were for this miracle.

3 - OH TO BE DORIS DAY!

"Que sera sera! Whatever will be, will be;
The future's not ours to see, Que sera sera!"
Song made popular by Doris Day;
Written by Jay Livingston and Ray Evans

I never really struggled with self-esteem issues growing up. I wasn't the prettiest girl in school. I wasn't the most popular. I wasn't the smartest. I wasn't the fastest. But I always had my voice, and singing helped me find my value. Infertility robbed me of it.

One negative pregnancy test led to the next ... and each time a little more of my self-worth went with it into the garbage can. Somewhere in the middle of my ache I came up with a new name for myself: "Old Worthless". At first I used it in gest, but it didn't take long for the name to stick in my spirit and I began to accept it as truth. As my self-worth hit rock bottom, words said to me in days gone by resurfaced in my memory to solidify my low self-esteem.

I remembered the times in grade school when kids would pick on me for my freckles or the way my behind wiggled when I walked (seriously!) or my outdated clothes. I remembered the time when my voice cracked while singing in a talent contest and a member of the audience (a regional celebrity) blurted out that her seven year old niece could sing better than me. I remembered the time when I got the leading role in "The Sound of Music" and some fellow cast mates said I was too fat to play Maria. All words ... but words hurt.

No words hurt as bad, though, as the words said to me by one of my most loved and respected relatives. We had just watched an old Doris Day movie and I was happily singing along to one of her tunes, when he said "Now that's who you should look like." Okay, I could have taken that. Don't we all want to look like Doris Day? But he took it a step further when he said, "You'll never get married. Nobody would ever want to marry you looking the way you do."

His words stung. In one 60 second exchange he had based my entire value as a woman on my outside appearance. It didn't matter to him that I had a generous spirit, a heart for God, or any kind of talent. The only thing that mattered was how I looked. I couldn't believe someone I loved so much could be so cruel.

At the time I brushed off his words and moved on with my life. The words were ignorant and harsh, but I didn't allow them to define me. If I wasn't loved because I didn't look like Doris Day, so be it. I wasn't set on marriage anyhow.

I always wanted to throw those words back at him when Greg asked me to marry him. It turned out he was wrong. Not only could someone love me for who I was – but he could find me beautiful inside and out. As I became "Old Worthless" though I started to relive those words in my memory.

Maybe he was right. Maybe I wasn't good enough. Maybe I wasn't worth having. Maybe Greg would be better off without me. I gave Greg permission to go and find someone else. "Find someone who can give you children. You deserve better than me," I told him.

Greg could only love me through these tough times. My value was no longer based on my talent. My value was not even based on my looks. My value, at least to me, was now based solely on the health of my ovaries and they were failing miserably.

Those were difficult times, and it has taken me some time to unpack those painful memories. I'll never be Doris Day, I'm sorry if that disappoints you. But then Doris Day will never be me either.

It has taken me some time to realize it, but even my ovaries can no longer define me. Psalm 139:14 says "I am fearfully and wonderfully made". If the Creator of the universe, the one who parted the Red Sea and shut the lion's mouth thinks I'm wonderfully made – then surely there must be more to me than what you see in the mirror ... or on a pregnancy test.

KARMEN BERNACCHI

4 - THE SHADOW OF DEATH

*"Yea, though I walk through the valley of the shadow of death,
I will fear no evil: for thou art with me;
Thy rod and thy staff they comfort me." – Psalm 23:4 (KJV)*

The first few years of our marriage our desire to be parents consumed our thoughts and our prayers. Nothing else seemed to matter. Then my Dad got sick. He was diagnosed with cancer and though he underwent chemotherapy and radiation, the doctors gave him little hope.

We had been through a lot with my Dad. About ten years earlier he had an aneurism on his brain. It was a miracle that he had survived it. He spent months in the hospital fighting back from the aneurism and a string of strokes that accompanied it.

It was a difficult time in our family. After my Dad's aneurism he could no longer work. With little savings and no way to meet their financial responsibilities my Mom had to come up with a way to secure their future. She decided to open a business caring for the elderly in her home. This allowed her to raise enough money to meet their responsibilities, and still take care of Dad. I so admired her determination and steadfastness. She had been through a lot with my Dad over the years and yet her loyalty and courage remained so strong.

It was difficult to watch my Dad suffer throughout those years. He had always been strong physically, and I guess in my naivety I thought he always would be. But the aneurism literally changed him into a different person. No longer was he a strong, independent provider. Instead he had turned into a fun-loving, jokester who could be both exasperating and hilarious all at the same time. He also had moments that scared us all to the core.

A few years after his aneurism he began experiencing a real imbalance in his brain chemistry. He started telling people that he was thinking of killing my Mother. My Mom grew very concerned and quite honestly frightened for her own safety. We were scared too. We knew he needed help, but he refused to get it. So my brothers and I got together and had him committed to a mental health facility. It was the hardest thing we ever had to do. It broke our hearts, but we knew we couldn't risk him hurting Mom and we knew it would be even more difficult on her if she had to commit him. In the end they adjusted his medication and he was eventually allowed to come home.

We were used to dealing with Dad's health issues, but watching him suffer with cancer was extremely difficult. His cancer was so progressive and occupied so much of his body that even touching him hurt. He couldn't eat. He had difficulty even drinking at times. The pain he experienced was insufferable.

Throughout his fight with cancer, Dad had an amazing disposition. We knew he was in great pain but he always had a smile and a joke to share. He didn't let the cancer rob him of his joy. That was something I admired so much and a quality I longed to have in my own life.

Towards the end of his fight we spent as much time with him as we could. We knew his time was growing short and we didn't want to have regrets. Unfortunately as we watched my father wither away, Greg's father became ill and died without warning.

We were stunned and overwhelmed with grief. We had not expected such a sad turn of events. Greg was devastated that he hadn't had the opportunity to say goodbye. Three weeks later, in the midst of our grieving, my Dad died.

I was sad, but prepared. Unlike Greg, I had the opportunity to say goodbye. I wanted him to stay, but I wanted him healed more than anything. We prayed every day that God would heal him, and while we had hoped it would take place here on earth, God chose to heal him by taking him to heaven. We trusted in His grace and were thankful he no longer had to suffer.

Losing my Dad at such a young age (59) was hard on our family and made me think of my own mortality. I wasn't ready to lose my Dad. I wanted him to be there for my children. I felt cheated that he would never bounce his grandchild on his knee. That he would never take them for a ride in his truck (that was a big deal to him!) That he would never slip money to them under the kitchen table. (Another big thing for him. Much to my mother's chagrin, Dad enjoyed giving all of his money away.)

Earlier I talked about how my father was never content. Finally he was. He had gone on to be with Jesus and there would be no more pain, no struggling. No more limitations from his physical body. No more wanting, he now had it all.

I know my Dad never accomplished everything he had set out to do. All of his dreams had not come true. But he had left a stamp on my heart and life and I would never forget him. I vowed then and there to make my life count for something. I wanted a baby more than anything but I couldn't stop living because we didn't have one. I had an amazing husband. I had a lifetime of opportunity waiting for me. It was time for me to stop pining away waiting to start a family and to start following my dreams.

Shortly thereafter Greg and I started pursuing one of our dreams by starting "Karmen & Greg Ministries." We realized that life was indeed short and we needed to get the gospel message out to as many people as we could while we still had time to do so. By utilizing

Christian drama, comedy and music we began building our ministry. My brother Kevin, who has also been one of our closest friends and supporters, joined us in the ministry as our sound technician and we began ministering in churches, coffee houses and festivals throughout the tri-state area.

KARMEN BERNACCHI

5 - LOST IN THE DARK

*"My God, my God, why have you forsaken me?
Why are you so far from saving me,
so far from the words of my groaning?" – Psalm 22:1*

In early 2001, we were contacted by one of our young relatives. She was pregnant. The unplanned pregnancy had quickly unraveled her already fragile world and she saw adoption as her only way out. She knew how badly we wanted a child and asked us if we would adopt her baby.

At first we were cautious. We knew this was a difficult decision and we didn't want her to have regrets down the road. She convinced us that she was sure of her decision and there was "no way" she was going to change her mind.

After a few weeks our caution gave way to enthusiasm as we began preparing for the baby's adoption. We contacted a lawyer and social worker and began taking the necessary steps to complete the adoption. We also started shopping and buying the things we would need for the baby.

We went to her doctor's appointments with her and heard the baby's heartbeat. We saw the ultrasound and were so excited to think that this child would one day be our son or daughter.

We were very torn between our compassion for the young mother's situation and our own excitement at the thought of becoming parents. We had waited so long for this day and we were sure that this was God's plan for our lives.

Though I'm sure we prayed about this child's adoption, I believe that our strong desire to be parents impaired our ability to hear from God, because a few months later our adoption plans came unraveled at the seams.

She never really told us that she had changed her mind. But we started seeing the signs that something had changed. She just stopped calling and returning calls. We knew in our hearts that something had changed. And we were heartbroken. Though we hadn't lost all hope, we knew that to preserve our financial future we needed to put the brakes on the legal aspects of the adoption. And so everything was put on hold.

A month or so later we heard from a family member that she had indeed changed her mind. We understood her change of heart. We wanted her to do what was best for her. And yet our hearts had been broken in two. In a way we had already bonded with the baby she was carrying in her womb, and we felt as though we had lost a child.

This failed adoption sent me into a very deep depression. There is no way for me to describe the darkness that settled over my soul, but I was totally lost in its grip. I cried day and night. I couldn't sleep at night. At times I felt like I couldn't breathe because of the grief that had grabbed hold of me. Months passed and I was still clawing to get out of the pit I found myself in.

Well-meaning friends and family members told us "it wasn't meant to be." Others just ignored our loss. I felt so alone and desperately wished we had never told anyone about our adoption plans.

About the same time I lost my job. After 15 years with the same company, I learned my position, along with about 125 other positions, were being eliminated. Since the age of 14 I had worked. I had never been without work for more than a week. I really didn't know what to do with my new-found unemployed status. All I knew was that with everything else going on in my life, the last thing I wanted to do was jump into another job right away. I needed time to think and heal and I viewed this time as a chance to do just that.

Though the uncertainty about our financial future was looming, I felt relieved not be working. Not having to go to work meant I didn't have to tell everyone at work what had happened. I also didn't have to try to put on a smile every morning. I was free to just hide out for a while. Whether that helped me or made things worse I really cannot say. But it did allow me some time to get through this difficult phase in our lives.

As the baby's due date neared I sunk further into the depression. I wanted desperately to end the pain and move on, but I was lost in the dark and I couldn't see any light.

We got a phone call when the baby was born. It was a girl. Everyone was very excited for the birth of this beautiful little baby. We understood that, yet we felt sad and forgotten. The depression only grew worse, and anger and bitterness started to set in my soul. I was mad at the baby's mother – not for keeping her baby – but for ever asking us to adopt her.

That anger and bitterness grew. It was like rust on an old car. It just grew worse and worse. And there was nothing I could do to get rid of that rust. I tried to cover it up when we were around others but it was eating me up inside and it was destroying my life.

A couple months after the birth of the baby, the girl called to ask if she could bring the baby by so we could see her. Greg invited her over. I didn't want to see that baby! I knew we couldn't avoid her forever, but I just wasn't ready.

Ready or not, the visit happened. Though I knew he was hurting too, Greg was able to set the pain aside knowing that this was a step we needed to take. I, however, was not ready to be so gracious. I was dying on the inside. I didn't want to look at the baby, let alone hold it. It wasn't the baby's fault, but it hurt so bad I simply couldn't see past the loss I'd experienced.

As I held the baby my body quaked and tears rolled down my cheeks. It was all I could do not to start sobbing. I was angry at myself for letting my emotions show. I was angry at the mother for putting me through that. Darkness enveloped me and I wanted to die.

As my heart and mind battled to survive this difficult encounter, I heard God speak to me. I'm not a person who claims to hear God's voice on a regular basis. I have sensed Him speaking to me on many occasions. I have felt His presence. I have experienced gentle urgings. But the times He has spoken loud and clear to me are few and far between.

How did I know it was God? John 10:27 says "My sheep hear my voice; I know them and they follow me." I knew it was Him ... it had to be. At this dark place in my life, I wouldn't have come up with these instructions on my own.

He told me to forgive her. Forgive her? I was hurt. I was angry. Sure I would forgive her in time, but I wasn't ready to. How could He ask that of me? Then, as if that wasn't enough, He told me to go upstairs and bring down everything I'd bought for the baby and give it to this young mother. No! How could God ask me to do that? I bought those items for our baby. I bought them for the child that was meant to be mine. I wrestled with His instructions and didn't want to do it.

As she prepared to leave that afternoon, I felt as though a force was literally pushing me off the couch, driving me to go up those stairs and start carrying down all of our accumulated baby gear and clothing. Though he didn't say anything at the time, Greg didn't know what had come over me. We then carried those things out and loaded them in her car.

As we placed the last load of things in her car, something happened. There is really no better way for me to explain it, other than to say it was like somebody turned the light on. That dark cloud of depression that had settled on my soul disappeared like a mist in the summer sun.

I realize now that while sadness and loss had naturally found its place in my heart, it was unforgiveness that kept me in depression's grip. Climbing those stairs and bringing down all of those baby things was a physical step I had to take. It wasn't about the stuff. It wasn't about the young mother. It was my physical act of forgiveness. It was my choice to let go of the bitterness that had enveloped me. And when I finally chose to take that step the healing came.

They say hindsight is always 20/20. If I had known then what I know now, I would have known that just like God's word promises,

"And we know that all things work together for good to them that love God, to them who are the called according to his purpose." -- Romans 8:28 (KJV).

That little girl belonged with her birthmother. That young mother would not have been able to live with her decision and would have had a lifetime of regrets. We wanted to be parents, but this was not the child for us.

Today that birthmother is like a daughter to me. I love her and cherish her place in our hearts and our family. And her daughter is like a granddaughter to us. We treasure them both. Though the road we all traveled seemed unbearable at the time, it did indeed work out for good, and we are stronger because of it.

Some other positive things came out of this journey as well. First, I learned the importance of forgiveness. In all honesty, I had no right to harbor unforgiveness towards this young mother. She was faced with an impossible decision, and had I been in her shoes I would have done the same thing. It hurt that she let us hang on for so long, but she loved us and knew how badly we wanted to be parents. I know she didn't want to be the cause of more pain.

Second, it opened our hearts towards adoption. We believed in adoption, but really didn't know if it was for us. Could we bond with a child that wasn't our own flesh and blood? With this baby we had bonded before she was even born. Biological or adopted we were ready to be parents and were willing to go down whatever path we needed to make that happen.

When I was a little girl my Mom and Dad used to recite a poem to me whenever I'd go through a disappointment. Written by Edith Lillian Young it is an excellent reminder that God has our best interests at heart, though it may not seem like it at the time.

"Disappointment -- His Appointment"
Change one letter, then I see
That the thwarting of my purpose
Is God's better choice for me.
His appointment must be blessing,
Tho' it may come in disguise,
For the end from the beginning
Open to His wisdom lies.

"Disappointment -- His Appointment"
Whose? The Lord, who loves me best,
Understands and knows me fully,
Who my faith and love would test;
For, like loving earthly parent,
He rejoices when He knows
That His child accepts, unquestioned,
All that from His wisdom flows.

"Disappointment -- His Appointment"
"No good thing will He withhold,"
From denials oft we gather

Treasures of His love untold,
Well He knows each broken purpose
Leads to fuller, deeper trust,
And the end of all His dealings
Proves our God is wise and just.

"Disappointment -- His Appointment"
Lord, I take it, then, as such.
Like the clay in hands of potter,
Yielding wholly to Thy touch.
All my life's plan in Thy molding,
Not one single choice be mine;
Let me answer, unrepining --
"Father, not my will, but Thine."

Over the next few years we would experience two more failed adoption attempts, but while we were very disappointed never again did I visit such a dark place.

6 - I SURRENDER

Trust in the LORD *with all thine heart;*
and lean not unto thine own understanding.
In all thy ways acknowledge him,
and he shall direct thy paths.
Proverbs 3:5-6

There's an old hymn by Judson W. Van DeVenter that has been a favorite of mine for many years. It's words:

All to Jesus I surrender; All to Him I freely give;
I will ever love and trust Him, In His presence daily live.

I surrender all, I surrender all;
All to Thee, my blessed Savior, I surrender all.

All to Jesus I surrender; Humbly at His feet I bow,
Worldly pleasures all forsaken; Take me, Jesus, take me now.

All to Jesus I surrender; Lord, I give myself to Thee;
Fill me with Thy love and power; Let Thy blessing fall on me.

I had sung that song since I was a little girl, and I thought I knew what surrender meant. But as I have sat in "God's Waiting Room" I have learned that it is easier to surrender some things to God than others.

Surrender to me meant "God I'm going to give this situation to you. Thank you so much for taking it from me. Whew! I feel better now. Okay, so now I'll go see about getting it done."

I believe there is a place and time for that "git 'r done" mentality. Sometimes you have to put feet to your faith. But I am learning that other times you need to say "Okay God, I can't do anything about this and everything I have tried to do in my own power has failed. This one is totally on you. I surrender control completely to you." And then you leave it there.

Greg is really good at that. He prays about it, lays it at Jesus feet and then waits for Him to bring it to pass. Me? Not so much. I'm a planner. I like to know what's going on. I like to be in control. But when you surrender something to God, you have to give Him the control – otherwise your surrender is no surrender at all. It is just words.

Eight years into our wait to start a family, it became painfully clear that my will and God's will were on different pages. We had done everything we could and all the planning in the world could not change our circumstances. It was time to let go – not of the dream – but of my need to control it.

We had been through a lot -- the loss of our fathers; the loss of the baby; the loss of a job. Our hearts were healing, and yet we still felt a little lost. It was time to refocus – a time to find a new direction for our family, even if it were only Greg, Lumpy (our cocker spaniel) and I.

We had always taken our vacations in the mountains. I could sit for hours at the edge of a vista, just staring at the majesty of the mountains. I love finding a brook or a waterfall in the middle of nature and listening to the steady, calming sound of water flowing across its smooth rocks. I love the smell of sage brush and the sound of rocks as they slip beneath my boots tumbling to the ground below. I love the sound of aspen leaves and a crackling fire on a cool autumn night. I love how close the stars are. The mountains soothe my senses and make me feel small – yet hopeful somehow.

Yet, we were entering a new chapter of our lives. We needed to make new memories. So we decided to go someplace new. We had two glorious weeks and decided to drive east. We booked a cabin on the ocean in Maine and took our time getting there. We viewed the wonder of Niagara Falls along the way. We were captivated by the rolling hills of upstate New York. We visited covered bridges in Vermont. We marveled at the beautiful mountains of New Hampshire. We smiled and laughed and dreamed about our future.

We took our dog Lumpy along and laughed that we had become one of those couples whose dog was treated better than most people's kids. He was. We took our time getting to our destination and looked forward to the picturesque setting that was waiting for us on the coast. Finally, 1600 miles and three days of driving later, we pulled up to our secluded cabin and quickly walked around to the deck to take in the beautiful ocean view we saw on the website.

Our enthusiasm quickly gave away to horror as we looked off the deck to find our ocean view was nothing but endless views of mud. There were no crashing waves. No seagulls on the shore. There was mud and dead fish. We could have heard more waves and spent a whole lot less money at the lake eight miles from our front door.

Weary from our journey we took some solace in the charming interior of the cabin, and determined that nothing was going to ruin this vacation. We were together and that was all that mattered. We would enjoy the tranquil serenity this secluded, wooded cabin offered and set our disappointment aside and just enjoy being together.

We unloaded the car and headed into town to pick-up supplies. We discovered the nearest town (which was about 18 miles away) was a bigger bust than the cabin. There were hardly any restaurants, no interesting landmarks and literally nothing to do. We bought enough groceries to hold us for a week, and headed back to the cabin to hideaway for a while.

As we pulled up to the cabin we were delighted to find that our mud hole had turned into a beautiful ocean while we were gone.

We'd never been to the ocean before. It was our first experience with the tides. Our ocean front cabin was ocean front – it just wasn't ocean front around the clock.

It struck me how much my own journey had mirrored that of the tides. When I got married it was definitely at the high tide of my life. We dove into our marriage excited about the future. We saw nothing but blue skies ahead. Disappointments and stormy seas, though, had our dreams stuck in the mud of low tide.

I realized that I could remain stuck there until the mud and sand buried me, or I could look to the tide that was sure to come in again if I held fast to my faith and didn't give up. That cabin was the setting for some beautiful devotionals as we sat on the deck watching the tide come and go. With each tide my faith strengthened.

As we headed home from our ocean retreat we paused long enough to take in a beautiful coastal town with wide open ocean views and magnificent coastal views. As Greg and Lumpy strolled along the ocean, I kicked off my shoes (despite cool fall temperatures) and waded in the freezing water.

Then I sat back in the sand, placed my hopes and dreams in my hand, and surrendered them back to God. And then I heard God speak to me. It wasn't a loud, booming voice. It was more of a whisper that rolled in with the waves. A whisper that said, "One day there will be a child for you across that ocean." And hope was born.

7 - BELIEVE ME NOW

"Never be afraid to trust an unknown future to a known God." – Corrie Ten Boom

A year later we were still holding on to hope. Still believing that God had a plan. Still dreaming of a family of our own. But still desperately lost when it came to making that dream come true. The cost of international adoption was just so high, and we simply did not have the money required to start that journey. So we sat – waiting; longing; with empty arms.

I began taking steps. I did research on the various countries open for international adoption. I looked at adoption agencies. I ordered materials and researched financial aid. I wanted to be as prepared as possible. We didn't know where we would get the money to start our journey, but we also knew it would never happen if we didn't start taking some steps.

Then our world was shook once again. We were preparing for a visit with Greg's mother, when we got the call. They found her in her bed. She was gone. She had been so healthy. So active in her retirement community. But out of the blue she was gone. And then out of the blue we were heartbroken. We didn't get to say "goodbye". We were going to see her the next day, but we were too late.

The next week was a bit of a blur as we planned her funeral, cleaned out her apartment and dealt with issues of the estate. Her death took Greg's whole family by surprise and the loss left another big hole in the Bernacchi family. After closing out her estate we realized that we would be receiving a financial settlement. We talked briefly about what we could do with the money ... pay off bills, buy a boat, invest it ... we knew, of course, there was only one place for that money for us.

We were crushed by her death. It was so sudden and so sad. We miss her terribly. And yet we owe her an enormous debt, because it is through the inheritance that she left us that we were able to pursue our dreams of adding to the Bernacchi family. For that we knew Mom Bernacchi would be proud.

We didn't waste any time moving forward with the adoption. We had waited so long. And I was well prepared. We set-up appointments with two home study agencies and began the process of selecting an agency.

The first agency we went to was my first choice on paper. But they were very slow and methodical to their approach. But we had enough "slow" in our lives. It was time to go! We selected another agency and were confident that they were much more sensitive of our desire to move quickly, and yet they warned us there could be some insurmountable roadblocks ahead for us.

China was looking at implementing a weight restriction for adoptive parents. After 11 years of praying to be parents, we could finally see the light at the end of the tunnel – but felt like it was a freight train ready to plow us down. My weight had plagued me my whole life. I was scared to death that my extra weight threatened to kill our dreams for a family.

I was driving to work the next morning, sure that once again our "baby" dreams were going to come up empty. I had Steven Curtis Chapman's "All Things New" CD in the player and the song "Believe Me Now" came on. As the music played, the lyrics spoke to me as though it were God himself talking to me. The words:

I watch you looking out across the raging water
So sure your only hope lies on the other side
You hear the enemy that's closing in around you
And I know that you don't have the strength to fight
But do you have the faith to stand and...

Believe Me now, Believe Me here
Remember all the times I've told you loud and clear

I am with you and I am for you
So believe Me now, Believe Me now
I am the One who waved my hand and split the ocean
I am the One who spoke the words and raised the dead
And I've loved you long before I set the world in motion

I know all the fears you're feeling now, But do you remember who I am?
I am the God who never wastes a single hurt that you endure;
My words are true, and all My promises are sure, so believe Me now ...

The song reminded me that God was not going to abandon us on this journey. He had breathed this dream into me. It was HIS dream too. I simply needed to <u>believe.</u>

One major thing that stood in our way was the extensive physical I would have to undergo ... and I was pretty worried about it. The last time I had been to the doctor my blood pressure had been elevated, and that, coupled with my weight, could be enough to end our adoption dreams.

I knew the blood pressure had to be good, so I took off work early that day so I could come home and have some "quiet time" before going in for my appointment. As I was reclined in my chair, listening to Bryan Duncan's "Quiet Prayers" on the CD player, I prayed that God would let my blood pressure be not only good, but that it would be really good. I asked God specifically to make it "like 120 over 76" ... that, I told Him, would be really good.

Little did I know that God was about to give me a little miracle and what I considered a sign that He was indeed in this. I went to the doctor and my blood pressure was 120 over 76. It was <u>exactly</u> what I'd prayed for! And God breathed into my soul – "Do you believe me now??"

8 - BLAZING THE PAPER TRAIL TO OUR DAUGHTER

"Saddle up your horses, we've got a trail to blaze,
Through the wild blue yonder of God's amazing grace.
Let's follow our leader into the Glorious unknown,
This is the life like no other, this is the great adventure."
– Steven Curtis Chapman

Most people that have adopted internationally would tell you how overwhelming it can be to adopt a child from outside of our borders. Many adoptive parents complain about all of the steps required, from writing detailed biographies of your life, to thorough background checks including FBI fingerprint clearance and so much more. I have known more than a few people who had minor breakdowns during this phase. Not me. I loved this part of our process. (Well most of it.)

With every single paper I completed; every time I wrote a check; every time I had something notarized and certified I rejoiced because we were one step closer to our daughter. Biologically expectant mothers have ultrasounds; adoptive parents give x-rays of our entire lives. Everything is brought into light from how you manage your finances, past relationships, medical concerns and more. They wanted to know every address we have lived at since we were 18 years old. Greg and I have lived pretty clean and uncomplicated lives so none of this bothered us too much.

I whizzed through this part of our process. What took most people 4 to 6 weeks took me about one week to complete. I worked diligently to make sure that our paperwork was filed as quickly as possible. Everything was going like clockwork, until the U.S. government was added to the mix.

Our final step before sending all of our paperwork to China was to file our application for advance processing of orphan petition (form I-600A) with the United States Citizen and Immigration Services (USCIS). Typically that took about three weeks to process. Which was two weeks too long if you ask me. I'd completed two inches of paperwork in one week, all they had to do was add a rubberstamp to one small form. There was no reason to hold it up. But hold it up they did.

105 days later we were still waiting for our "golden paper" -- the I-171H. One would think with all the waiting I had done over the years, this should be nothing to me. But I was going out of my mind. What was taking so long???

Finally I reached my "waiting" limit, and requested the assistance of Senator Herb Kohl in trying to find out why the USCIS was taking so long. Three days later we had our approval, and were able to send our paperwork off to our agency to prepare it for China.

I knew that God's timing was critical in this whole process ... and I didn't want to rush out ahead of where we were predestined to be in the process, but we had been waiting to be parents for 11 years and quite simply, I was getting tired of waiting! Little did I know the wait was just getting started.

On September 11, 2006 our paperwork was officially "logged in" with the China Center of Adoption Affairs. 9-11. It seemed almost surreal that the day that would forever be remembered for its tragic loss of life, had new meaning for us as we had finally found our place in line for a child to call our own.

Five years earlier I was sitting in a college marketing class when we heard the World Trade Center had been attacked. The teacher got up and explained what was going on. At the time all I wanted to do was get to a radio and hear my husband's voice. Greg was the morning host on our local radio station, and I knew I'd feel better hearing him read the news that day than anyone else. Unfortunately, my teacher decided to turn the class into a lesson on crisis marketing instead. Not a bad idea - I suppose – but the last thing I wanted to think about at that time was marketing!

That day changed the world forever. Our comfortable existence was tarnished by the cruel reality of a world filled with evil. Some of my friends and family said that they wouldn't want to bring up children in this new world. The world has gotten mean and hard and unfit. It's true the world is full of evil, but hasn't it always been? What about Nero who lit his courtyard with Christians whom he burned at the stake. What about Adolf Hitler and his horrific rule. Good "Christians" used to enslave people just because of the color of their skin. No, people haven't really changed.

There has always been evil. There will always be evil ... it's just changing it's disguise. I can't help but think what this world would be like if Abraham Lincoln's parents would have decided that the world was too cruel to raise a son in ... would we still have slavery? What if Winston Churchill and FDR's parents had decided to forego having kids ... would Hitler have been successful in his annihilation of the Jews?

From the very beginning of our prayers for a little one, I had asked God to give me a "world changer". I prayed for a child who would stand up for what is right, a child that would make a difference.

9-11 is a tragic day in our country's history. But for one middle-aged couple in Mauston, Wisconsin , 9-11 had new meaning ... for it was the "official" date that we were logged-in for our future "world changer". Our "official" wait had just begun.

9 - BASKET WEAVING

"Forsaking All I Trust Him" – *Pastor James Gast*

Shortly after we began the process to adopt from China, our Pastor felt like he had a word from God for us that "our faith would weave the basket that would carry our child home to us." Little did we know at the time just how crucial our faith would be in this process.

When we started the process to adopt, the wait time for a healthy child was 9 to 12 months from the time your paperwork was logged in. By the time we were logged in that wait time had increased to 15 months and that wait time continued to grow.

Each month the wait lengthened just a little bit more. The increased wait time was credited to many things. China had a one-child policy at the time we were in process (they have since relaxed those laws), but citizens that had more than one child had to pay a hefty fine to the Chinese government. An improved economy made paying this fine within reach to more Chinese people. So there were fewer child abandonments. Domestic adoption was reportedly on the rise as well. These were good things – but for us it meant a longer process.

Then scandal broke out. There were reports of corruption in the Hunan province. This brought China's international adoption program to a screeching halt. Suddenly the wait time went from 15 months to two to three years, and everything pointed to it just getting worse.

Four years later we found ourselves still waiting with no end in sight. Our friends and family were growing weary of the process. A lot of well-meaning people who simply knew how bad we wanted to be parents, kept coming up with other adoption options for us. We'd been told countless stories about Ethiopia, Vietnam, and had been told of a whole bunch of domestic opportunities. So many people tried to discourage us from staying on this course. "It's never going to happen." "They're just stealing your money." "Are you sure you know what you're doing?"

Keeping our faith alive as our adoption support waned was really tough. One particularly difficult evening, I went to the altar at church and just wept. I felt so abandoned by God. So forgotten. So desperate. I was hoping God would speak some audible word that would give me hope for the future or something ... But alas, no grand word was written on the wall, no thunderous voice told me that things in China would change and we would be united with our child by such and such a date ... We did however get a hug from a friend who said "Jesus says it will be alright ..."

As I considered the journey we were on and whether we were indeed wasting our time, our Pastor's word about faith stuck in my heart. Pastor James Gast (my pastor in my teen years) translated faith, "<u>F</u>orsaking <u>A</u>ll <u>I</u> <u>T</u>rust <u>H</u>im". I knew that was the kind of faith that we needed to have for this journey, because if we looked at the numbers alone, the impossibility of the situation would have caused us to give up. Many waiting families were throwing in the towel, pursuing other adoptive routes, or just giving up on their adoption dreams all together. But despite the discouraging reports from China there was one thing we knew for certain. We were supposed to be on this road to China. We believed that with all of our hearts. And even if the wait was 5 years or more ... we were determined to keep our eyes focused on the vision God had given us for our family.

Joshua Zhong, the Director of our adoption agency -- Chinese Children Adoption International, sent us a letter that encouraged us greatly during the wait. In the letter he told the following story:

Florence May Chadwick was an American swimmer who in 1950 was the first woman ever to swim the English Channel both ways. Two years later, Florence decided to take up the challenge to swim the 26 miles between Catalina Island and the California coastline.

Hour after hour Florence swam, but after 15 hours, a thick, heavy fog set in. Florence began to doubt her ability and became discouraged. She struggled to swim for one more hour. Emotionally exhausted, she asked to be pulled out of the chilly water. As the fog gave way, Florence saw that she had stopped swimming just one mile from the California shoreline, her destination! Florence explained later that she quit because she could no longer see the coastline - there was too much fog. She had lost sight of her goal.

Two months later, Florence got back in the water to try again. This time was different. She swam from Catalina Island to the California shore in a straight path for 26 miles. The same thick fog set in, but this time she made it! She succeeded because, as she shared, she kept a mental image of the shoreline while she swam. She never allowed herself to lose the image of her goal.

In Romans 4 Paul discusses the faith of Abraham who *"did not weaken in faith when he considered his own body (since he was about 100 years old) or when he considered the barrenness of Sarah's womb. No distrust made him waver concerning the promise of God, but he grew strong in his faith as he gave glory to God, fully convinced that he was able to do what He had promised."*

Greg and I chose to stand on that faith -- not on the circumstances -- believing that God was fully able to break down walls in China and bring our baby home to us.

It was scary. Sometimes we felt like "taking matters into our own hands" and jumping outside of God's perfect plan for us. But we were determined to wait on God's timing and trust that He would not let us down.   All the while that faith was weaving that basket that would one day soon carry our Ella home to us.

10 - ENOUGH!

"But my God shall supply all your need according to His riches in glory by Christ Jesus." -- Philippians 4:19 (KJV)

As the wait time continued so did the financial concerns I had over our adoption. Though the majority of the finances were provided for through an inheritance -- we still had some funds to raise. And our needs only grew as the wait time grew. Fees were increasing. Paperwork expired and had to be renewed. The U.S. dollar weakened. It seemed every time we turned around we needed more money for something.

Early on in this VERY LONG process my cousin and her husband had given us a considerable gift towards our adoption which was an extreme blessing! We tucked it away in a CD so that we would have it when we needed it. The gift was a real sacrifice for them and at times I felt guilty holding on to that money, knowing they could really use it and it was just sitting in the bank for years. But I knew they wanted to sow into our dream.

There were other gifts along the way as well. Gifts from family and friends. Money from strangers that had heard of our journey. Friends that bought magazine subscriptions from our website knowing the proceeds went to our adoption account. Little blessings that helped to build our faith.

Still I worried. And worry turned to fear. That fear began to consume me. What if we couldn't come up with the money? What if our dream dried up just like our bank account? I thought about it day and night. I was losing sleep. It was consuming my life.

Then one Sunday at church, some dear friends handed us a card and told us that we had been in their hearts and they wanted to do something for our baby. I thanked them. No matter what was in the card, it was a real blessing to know that someone else was thinking of our dream too. I had a suspicion that there might be some money in the card. I kind of thought it might be $25, maybe even $50.

I waited to open the card until we got in the car. The card was signed "Love, Jesus" and inside was a check for $3,000.

My whole life I have heard people say that God spoke to them. I believe that. In John 10:27 it says *"My sheep hear my voice ..."* I have heard God whisper to my heart before. I have felt his gentle nudging, but I have never heard him more loud and clear than I did that day. In fact, the voice was so loud, I asked Greg if he heard it too. The voice was stern and very clear. It said, "ENOUGH! I will not have you worrying about this anymore!"

I was overcome with the gift and overwhelmed with God's faithfulness. The gift was amazing, and a tremendous sacrifice for this couple. It was a huge blessing that went a long way in making our dream come true. But I think more than anything else it cemented my faith for the long journey ahead. Because of that gift I knew. This was God's dream. This baby was God's gift to us and HE was going to take care of it. And He did. Every single penny came in. Sometimes just in the nick of time. But it was there. God provided, and it was a great lesson in faith for us.

KARMEN BERNACCHI

11 - LOVE NEVER GIVES UP

"Love is patient ..." -- *I Corinthians 13:4 (NIV)*

While our thoughts were continuously consumed with our adoption process, the world around us continued to move forward. Years, literally, passed and it was no secret to anyone that we were still childless.

One particular weekend we had attended the Moore family reunion. The reunion is an annual event that has been taking place every year since before I was born. As expected, there were lots of questions like "When are you going to get your baby?" And others like "Don't you wonder if this is really worth it?" "Have you thought maybe you should just give up?" and the ever present, "China is just ripping you off!"

I knew I would hear those questions. For those that saw us year after year still holding on to a dream of our child, but not holding on to a child, it was hard to understand. I knew it seemed like it would never happen -- and at our age it may have seemed more appropriate for us to just "get on with our lives."

On a hot July evening, in 2008, I rushed home from our reunion to lead worship at church. At that service a dear friend, Elaine Hansen, spoke and her words echoed through my soul for days following. She talked about how Abraham was 100 years old and Sarah was 89 years old when God fulfilled his promise of a child. (Thank God He didn't wait that long with us ... I don't think I could have been that old and chased a toddler!) Surely people thought they were crazy too, but they held on to that dream and God's promise to them and they are the parents of many nations today.

One of the other things she spoke about was love, and though I've read the verse a million times, it really struck my heart that night. I Corinthians 13:4 says "Love is Patient". I looked it up in a couple of different translations and it said "Love suffers long," "Love endures long," and "Love never gives up."

As I thought about our journey to that point ... I realized it was more than just a journey about us wanting to become parents (although that certainly was a big part of it) ... this was a journey about a little child that would one day be found lying beside a busy street. Her parents would be unable to raise this child. This child would be abandoned, alone in this world, with no hope of a future unless someone were to take that child in. That child would need the love of a parent. That child would need the love of someone who is patient, suffers long, endures long, and never gives up. That child would need all the love I could give.

I loved that child already with my whole heart. I loved that child enough to be patient, to endure long, to suffer long, and to never give up during the long wait. My child deserved that kind of love -- and that's the kind of love I was determined to give my child.

Our adoption journey was a journey of love -- and that I Corinthians love is the kind of love the journey required. God placed an incredibly deep and long-suffering love in our hearts for a child halfway around the world that would need the love of a couple like us ... and so this couple vowed to NEVER GIVE UP.

KARMEN BERNACCHI

12 - FIGHTING FOR LIFE

*"Not by might nor by power, but by my Spirit,'
says the LORD Almighty." – Zechariah 4:6(NIV)*

On January 18, 2011 I woke up from a dream. A dream that was so real I woke up shaking and weeping. In my dream God told me that our daughter was fighting for her life somewhere in China and it was time for us to start fighting too. Never before or since have I had a dream that felt so real.

I told Greg that I really felt God had spoken to me in this dream. After sharing my dream we agreed to take the next week and really pray for our daughter.

Later that week Greg told me he felt like we were supposed to fill out the special needs checklist. WHAT? That made no sense. We had waited 5-1/2 years for a healthy child. We were less than a year away from our referral. Why would we change course now?

We were scared to death. We felt totally unprepared to raise a child with special needs. But we prayed over it, checked off a few needs we thought we could handle, and mailed it in to our adoption agency. We continued to pray for our child in the weeks ahead but pretty much forgot about the checklist. We were simply looking forward to the referral we knew was getting closer, special needs or not.

Six months later, on June 22, 2011 at 3:45 p.m. I was sitting at my desk at work when the phone rang. It was our adoption agency. They told me they had a little girl that they thought would be perfect for our family. "Would you like to see some pictures?"

I was crying and shaking so hard I could hardly open the email. For years I watched the website, knowing that it was a very systematic process. Everything went in a specific order and we would know when to anticipate the call. But this threw us total off kilter. We did not expect the call at all.

She was a beautiful little girl. 22 months old. She had a "minor" heart condition and some delayed development, but that was likely due to her institutionalized setting. They sent us her health records and more background on her, and asked that we make a decision within the next day or two.

I sat at my desk a little shell shocked, when the phone rang again. It was Greg. He was just leaving a tradeshow when photos of this beautiful little Chinese girl came up on his phone. "What are these? Is she ours??"

I gave him details of the call and we both raced home as quickly as we could to study the file and share the moment we had dreamed of for so many years. We were about to be parents ... or at least we hoped so!

We forwarded her health records to 3 doctors and each one told us the same thing -- from everything they can see in her health records, she appears to be overall healthy, and the heart issue was not something that was life threatening -- in fact it was likely that the small ASD would actually correct itself.

That was just the news we wanted to hear. We called our adoption agency and said, "Yes! We believe little Li Si Han of Pingdingshan, Henan, China is meant to be part of our family! We want to bring her home!" And so we officially accepted the referral. We were so excited!

Concentration on the job was nearly impossible the next few days. All I could think about was our sweet little girl that was waiting for us somewhere in China. "Somewhere in China. Somewhere in China." My mind had been such a blur when the phone call came in, I knew that I had missed details from that call.

I dug through the papers on my desk and found a scrap of paper I had taken notes on when the call came in. It had a place called

Morning Star Family Home in Beijing written on it. I didn't remember that part of our conversation, but knew they mentioned she was in foster care currently. Maybe this was where she was?

My fingers flew to Google and I did a quick search on Morning Star Family Home Beijing China and there she was. Our daughter's face was on the front page of this group foster home for orphans with heart conditions. Next to her picture it had the name "Joy" and said that she had Down syndrome.

My heart raced. My body shook. My stomach fell into my shoes. Down syndrome? No! That wasn't on the paperwork? We knew she had some developmental delays, but nothing like this! How could this be? We had said yes to some minor special needs, but we weren't prepared for this.

We had already said "yes" to the file. Now what do we do? I called Greg and then called the adoption agency right away. I told them what we'd found on the website, and they were as baffled as we were. Nothing in the paperwork indicated Down syndrome, and yet that is what the foster home said she had. We needed to know for sure.

Our paperwork was just about to leave the office for China, so they put a hold on it to investigate further. With one call to the foster home they learned that indeed they did suspect her of having Down syndrome -- though that had never been confirmed. She had never been tested. So our adoption agency ordered some genetic testing on her.

While we KNEW beyond a shadow of a doubt we could love this little girl -- we already did -- we were terrified at the thought of raising a child with such high special needs.

Our hearts were aching. We had told our friends and family. We had showed people her picture. I had made 8 X 10's and had them displayed all over our home and my office. How could we turn down this beautiful child now? And yet, that nasty fear bug was gripping me like never before.

We got a ton of advice and words from well-meaning folks. Some told us that if we had a biological child we could not choose if she had Down syndrome, and we would raise her -- and so we should do the same with this child. Others told us that we had waited too long and had too many dreams for our child to accept a child that is less than perfect.

Greg and I were not looking for a perfect child. We were just looking for a child that was perfect for us. And that we could be the perfect parents for. We just wanted to give a child the home they needed in order to thrive and be all they could be and to grow into an adult that is a "world changer" -- no pressure!

Six weeks later we were still awaiting results from the chromosome tests that had been ordered. It was the hardest part of our wait to become parents by far. I found myself wondering if God had delayed the tests for a reason. Were we hearing His voice? Was she really meant to be our daughter?

I was sitting at my desk, my stomach all tied up in knots, staring at a photo of little Li Si Han on my desk, when God spoke to me again through yet another Steven Curtis Chapman song. I knew it was Steven singing – but the message could not have been more clear to me. The lyrics pierced my soul.

I saw the face of Jesus in a little orphan girl
She was standing in the corner on the other side of the world
And I heard the voice of Jesus gently whisper to my heart
Didn't you say you wanted to find me?
Well here I am, here you are

So, What now? What will you do now that you found Me?
What now? What will you do with this treasure you've found?
I know I may not look like what you expected
But if you remember this is right where I said I would be
You've found me, what now?

"In as much as you've done for the least of these my brethren, you've done it unto Me." – Matthew 25:40. I was looking at the face of Jesus. He was in this little orphan girl.

God had given us this little girl. She was not perfect. She had a ton of question marks. But she was God's first choice for us. What were we going to do? The choice was ours. I knew then and there, that whether Li Si Han had Down syndrome or not, God was asking us to adopt THIS little girl. And we said "yes". "Yes" to the unknown. "Yes" to the question marks. "Yes" to this beautiful little girl that needed a Mommy and needed a Daddy.

The next day we got the call. The tests had come back. Li Si Han did not have Down's syndrome. Needless to say we were thrilled. And the weeks that led up to that conclusion seemed like such a waste of time. We couldn't understand why God would allow us to go through such a painful process – unless perhaps He was just looking for our obedience?

We knew there were still question marks surrounding this little girl, but also knew she was meant to be part of our family and we moved full speed ahead.

The next few weeks flew by as we finalized our paperwork, tied up loose ends at work and prepared to travel to bring home our daughter. Our Pastor gave a message about "speaking to the mountain" in our lives. Jesus said that we could say to that mountain be moved and it would fall into the sea. So, Greg and I resolved to speak to the mountain of paperwork that was keeping us from our daughter and that mountain was indeed moved.

We received our LOA (Letter of Acceptance -- basically our official documents from China) in just 14 days. A few weeks later we received our travel approval and we were packing our bags for China.

Our adoption agency sent us final paperwork that we would need to take with us on our journey. As we studied the file, something jumped off the page at us. Back in January when I had the gripping dream about our child fighting for her life, a little girl named Li Si Han's files were being added to the international adoption database. Her files were being processed by the CCAA on that VERY SAME DAY!

God knew that our little girl was finally ready to be adopted. And the fact that her paperwork made its way to our agency's dedicated list was nothing short of a miracle. Then to top it off, the fact that our agency matched her with our family was also a miracle.

Li Si Han was the Ella we had prayed for for so many years, and she was our little miracle! We believe that when God spoke to me in the dream, that she was indeed fighting -- fighting for the life that God had planned for her. She was our little miracle!

13 - TIME TO COME HOME!

*"There is a joy in the journey,
There's a light we can love on the way.
There is a wonder and wildness to life,
And freedom for those who obey."*
— Michael Card

Our day had finally come. It was time to board a plane and meet our little girl. I was excited ... we had waited for this day for so long. We had dreamed about how it would be when she was finally in our arms. When the little girl we have prayed for since before she was conceived finally made her way to her forever family. We knew this would be the journey of a lifetime.

I was scared ... would I be a good Mom? We were about to turn our worlds upside down! Greg and I had a great life together ... how would a child change the dynamic in our home? What about the trip? I was terrified of that part. I do not enjoy airline travel and I knew I would be in airports all over the world, with more luggage than the two of us could really handle ... could we survive the physical aspects of the trip?

I was sad ... sad for my little girl who was about to say goodbye to her friends and foster family in China. She had become very attached to these wonderful people. They saved her life and had loved her and given her every adoptive parent's dream -- a beautiful home until her forever family could bring her home. I knew Ella would experience grief and loss -- and would not understand what was happening. I was sad to put her through that.

I was overwhelmed ... by the love and support our families and friends had shown us. So many people had been excited for us and prayed for us and given us gifts. Our dear friends had thrown us an amazing shower and after years of painful "shower related" memories, I felt so loved and embraced on that special day.

I was happy ... my dream of becoming a Mom was finally coming true. So much about the journey had been hard; but every single hard day had led us to that moment. It was time. It was time to bring Ella home.

We boarded a plane in Chicago and 21 hours later (after a short stop in Tokyo) we arrived in Beijing, China. The next morning we met Bill and Lynsay Lewis, the founders of the Morning Star Family Home, where Ella had spent most of her life. They took us out to a very delicious, authentic Chinese lunch and then we made our way to the home to meet our little girl and see where she had lived for the past 14 months.

We were thrilled to meet Ella. She was not so thrilled to meet us. It wasn't that she had anything against us, she was just too busy playing to take time for these people that for some odd reason wanted to smother her with attention.

We spent several hours there loving on the children and talking with the Lewis family. It was SO great for us to be able to ask questions and learn more about our daughter. We learned more about her heart condition and delays. We left feeling grateful and confident that our daughter was not only well cared for, but loved. God placed her in an amazing home and we were so grateful.

People talk about our faith in this long journey, but our adoption journey ended when we got Ella. The Morning Star folks are in it every day for the long haul, until every last child has a forever family. We were inspired by their dedication.

The next day was a full day for all of us. Ella had to travel by train back to her home province in Henan, where she could "officially" meet us. Our meeting at Morning Star was strictly off the books. We had a fun day of touring Beijing.

As our driver took us around that massive city, I couldn't help but wonder what Ella's life would have looked like if she had stayed in China. Without a family support system what would have become of her?

There are millions and millions of people in Beijing. We were overwhelmed by the crowds. How could one orphaned girl make her way successfully in that city? The fact that she also had special needs would undoubtedly make the situation even more difficult. Chinese people have to pay cash in advance for any medical treatment. She would never be able to do that.

We did not set out on this journey to rescue an orphan. To be honest, we just wanted to be parents. But the further along we traveled on our journey the more I realized the spiritual significance to what we were doing. God has called each of us to care for orphans ... I know that not everyone can go and adopt. But there are so many that could at least give to help someone adopt ... or help homes like Morning Star that are making such a difference in the lives of orphaned children. Adoption is something we all should be part of in one way or another.

The next morning we prepared to make the trek to Zhengzhou in the Henan province where we would finalize her adoption.

As we arrived in Zhengzhou, I was really struck by the poverty and hard living the people of that city face. There is just so much we take for granted in the United States. It's the little things that made me appreciate where I live. For instance:

- I can walk on the sidewalk without fear of being struck by a motorcycle or scooter.
- I can use a public restroom and reach over to find toilet paper -- I was not so lucky at the Zhengzhou airport. You have to bring your own most places in China.
- I can flush the toilet paper down the toilet. You can't in China. You have to put it in the waste basket -- even in our "five star" hotel.
- I can turn on the air-conditioner in my room and cool off. It was hot in Zhengzhou, but the hotel had no air-conditioning during that time of year.

For years I had studied the process of adopting a child from China. I stewed over each thing and worried about stupid stuff that involved my own American comforts. As we anticipated the adoption of our daughter, I resolved that none of that really mattered.

The mattresses were hard. The food didn't sit well with me. It was hot. The bathroom situation was unique. But I just kept reminding myself that I didn't come to China to sleep. I didn't come to China to eat. I didn't come to China to use nice bathrooms or toilet paper (and I actually got pretty accomplished at the squatties, thank you very much!) This journey was all about a little girl who needed a home, and a childless couple who really just wanted to be a Mom and Dad.

And then came Gotcha Day. The housekeeping staff delivered a crib to our room about 30 minutes before we were to board the bus and travel to the Registration Office where we would be presented with our baby girl. As I looked at the crib, I was flooded with emotions. Joy, fear, excitement, panic ... it all rushed over me. Our lives were about to change forever.

We waited at the Registration Office for what seemed like forever, as one by one precious children were delivered to the other families in our travel group. Finally the moment we had been waiting for for so many years was upon us. The orphanage worker brought our little girl to us. She didn't cry (maybe because she'd met us just a couple days earlier.) She seemed to study us and kept hugging me tight and pressing her little head into my cheek. It was sweeter than any Gotcha moment I had ever seen.

Well, except she arrived in a very smelly fashion. She had gotten carsick on the ride from Pingdingshan and was covered in vomit. That didn't keep us from loving on her, but we were ready to get her back to the hotel for a much needed bath.

Ella did great all day, but her energy level was WAY more than we anticipated. She was just a little energizer bunny all day. So we played with her and kept her really busy. Finally we ended up at the swimming pool where we really discovered her great love for water. There was no napping for her, but we felt a real sense of relief when she finally drifted off just before dinner. And then the honeymoon period ended.

She woke about an hour later screaming her head off. She hadn't cried all day, but when she woke up she must have realized she was in a strange place with strange people ... and she didn't like it one bit. We didn't think she would ever quit crying, but finally she wore herself out and fell asleep.

The next morning we went back to the Registration Office and finalized our adoption in China. At that point it would have been a crime for us to abandon our child. She was ours. Then we headed to the Notary Office to finalize the paperwork for Ella's passport. We climbed to the top of this smoke filled building (everyone smokes in China) -- 6 floors up (20 stairs per flight ... I counted) no elevator. When you're not used to carrying a toddler and all their gear that is quite a feat. We were both ready for a nap ... Ella, however, was not.

We were relieved to have the adoption complete. But it was also an emotion filled couple of days. The highs had been very high ... we were finally parents to a beautiful little girl and we were so in love with her. Though there were also some pretty low lows, based somewhat on exhaustion I am sure.

The next few days were filled with Ella meltdowns. We know now that Ella does not handle change well, but at the time we simply did not know how to make our child happy. Other parents in our group were going through similar experiences, but all were experienced parents who seemed to take it all in stride. I, however, was a wreck! At one point I found myself locked in the hotel bathroom sitting on the side of the tub, just sobbing. I couldn't do this! What had I got myself into? It was too hard. I was sure that was the reason God hadn't given us children. It was too much for me. I couldn't handle it. I begged God for a way out. I just wanted to jump on a plane and go home. I was just so tired.

The next day we prepared to leave Zhengzhou for Guangzhou where we would finalize our paperwork at the United States Consulate's office. Everyone told us we would love Guangzhou and so we were hopeful that maybe a change of scenery would bring us more peace in our expanded little family.

Sadly the toughest part of our journey, at least for me, was still ahead. When we were in the airport, Greg went to check our bags, and I stayed with Ella. Ella did not like Daddy being gone one bit and had a complete melt-down. Here we were in public and she is wailing uncontrollably. And I was her Mommy! I felt like I should know what to do! But I didn't. I was a mess!

I took her out of her stroller and tried to console her. I held her. Danced with her. Offered her toys and treats ... but there was simply no consoling her. As she melted down, so did I. Right in front of all of my travel mates. I felt so lost. So scared. So alone. Finally one of our travel mate's children, ten year-old Ally, offered to take her for me. Immediately Ella stopped crying. I was so relieved, and yet somehow devastated at the same time. Why couldn't I give her what she needed? What was wrong with me?

The plane ride to Guangzhou was another major challenge. Ella was a very active child. Her legs and arms and voice never stop, and that was quite a handful on the plane. Fortunately the Chinese man sitting next to us spoke English and was really a kind person. He was from Ella's hometown -- Pingdingshan – and he told us just what a lucky girl Ella was to be adopted, and how badly he wished he could leave China.

After another meltdown, Ella finally fell asleep and we were both very relieved. When we arrived in Guangzhou, Greg carried Ella through the airport, through the hotel and to our room. She never woke up. She was so tired. Pretty sure, though, she wasn't as tired as I was.

The next morning we had a doctor appointment and spent some time strolling around Shamian Island. For years I had studied all the amazing shops on the island and I had such high hopes for great shopping, instead Ella was in meltdown mode once again and we found ourselves eager to get back to the hotel where we could just try to work through the situation in private.

We began to see that there was some sort of correlation between stimulation and Ella's meltdowns. She didn't do well when we were in high traffic areas. If there were lots of people and lots of noise we could most certainly expect a major meltdown. So while we had hoped to participate in tourist activities, we resorted instead to low key activities at our hotel as we got to know each other better and prepared to bring her home.

The next day we took the oath at the U.S. Consulate office and received Ella's approval to travel home. I couldn't help but tear up as we took the oath. In fact, I could only say the oath under my breath because I was busy choking back the tears. This had been such a LONG, LONG journey. It was hard to believe that we were finally at the end of this chapter and moving on to the start of the next.

After the oath ceremony, we went to the Guangzhou Safari -- a wonderful zoo with lots of panda bears and other beautiful animals. I was so worried about how Ella would do as the stimulation had been such a problem -- but she did very well at the zoo. She took a nap on the way there and didn't have a single meltdown the whole time we were there.

The next day we received our visas and hired a van to take us from Guangzhou to Hong Kong. It was a long 3-1/2 hour ride in traffic that you would not believe! We drove in three lane traffic, which is most of the times four or five cars wide, I don't know how else to describe it, but people didn't drive in the lanes .... it was complete chaos!

To make matters worse, Ella was like a wild cat the whole trip. With no car seat, Greg tried to hold her the best he could, but it was kind of like trying to harness the wind. Meanwhile our driver talked on his cell phone, put addresses in the GPS, read notes, talked on the radio ... and I was convinced that if we made it to the hotel it would be a miracle ... but we did and we were so glad we did!

The following day we boarded a plane and prepared for a 22 hour flight home. The first few hours of the flight Ella did pretty good. She was squirrely but we had an extra seat and that helped a lot. But then she got tired and started to cry ... and SCREAM ... as we had become accustomed to in China. Her cries invoked such helpless feelings within me.

As she screamed her heart out, one passenger took it upon herself to come to us and give us parenting advice ... "Did you try to walk with her? Have you given her a bottle? Have you sang to her? You have to do something! You can't let her scream like that!" This, of course, led to another Mommy meltdown too. As Ella cried, so did I until my eyes were swollen from the tears. Finally, I did the unthinkable. I put a little melatonin in her formula and she fell asleep within five minutes. She then slept for the next 7 hours, which was a HUGE blessing! Unfortunately, we did not sleep, so by the time we got to Chicago she was ready to go, and we were ready to crash.

In Chicago, Greg's sister Sue and her husband Tom and two of their friends (Candy & Mike) met us at the airport with flowers, welcome home balloons and gifts. Sue thought of everything, giving us a care package to carry us through our first few days, complete with energy drinks, comfort foods and simple convenience items.

The biggest comfort was just being surrounded by our family. It was such a real relief to have them there, as we couldn't imagine trying to get the shuttle at O'Hare when we were so tired we were literally shaky. They took us and all of our luggage to our car and then out for a bite to eat.

After we ate we talked about getting a hotel for one more night since we were so tired, but Greg really wanted to get home ... and while I was simply too shaky and weak to drive, he pushed through it and got us all home safe. Adrenaline? Maybe. Or maybe it was the screaming child in the back seat that literally screamed for three hours on our way home.

In China they don't use car seats and she did not like being restrained one bit. While it hurt us to see her cry that way, it was also a major relief to have her safe in her car seat, in our car, in our home state and headed home to try to somehow turn these three tired, sad, scared, overwhelmed people into a family.

The biggest relief I have ever felt came over me as we drove into our driveway. My eyes immediately flooded with tears as we looked at the most beautiful display of balloons and banners and decorations all welcoming Ella and the Bernacchi family home. We felt as though we had been given the biggest embrace of our lives. (We know now that it was our friends Tom and Mary Jane that left us that sweet embrace. They will never know how much that meant to us.)

We were greeted by our two puppies Chewy and Princess who were no worse for the wear, and a refrigerator full of goodies and a delicious meal which was such a tremendous blessing at the end of such a long, long journey.

We love China. China gave us our daughter. We wanted so badly to spend more time exploring it and understanding the culture more and seeing the beauty of it ... We saw a few things. We got out and about a little. But most of our time was spent getting to know our daughter, and helping her cope with the changes in her life.

We knew there would be much more coping to come. She was not done grieving ... her moods told us that. She had not fully attached to us yet, and we knew that it would take time. We had a long ways to go. But we were home, and ready to start the next chapter of our lives as a family.

KARMEN BERNACCHI

14 - A NEW NORMAL

*"Every day I look to You, to be the strength of my life.
You're the hope I hold on to be the strength of my life."*
-- Leslie Phillips

It was hard to believe that after 5-1/2 years of waiting in the China program (and 16 years of waiting to be parents) we were finally home with our Ella and the next chapter of our journey had begun.

Getting Ella to sleep became our greatest frustration ... day or night she simply did not want to sleep. She didn't just cry, she screamed and screamed and screamed. Motherhood was not at all like I had envisioned it would be. For some reason I had this perfect little fantasy, where my little girl would snuggle up on my lap and want me to hold her and read her stories and tuck her into bed. Ella was not like that at all.

Ella was always on the go -- always into something she shouldn't be. She was mischievous. She was naughty. She tested every ounce of my patience. I loved her with all my heart, but there were moments when I had to give myself a "time out" so that I didn't come unglued.

Ella was learning how to be part of a family, and we were learning to be parents. For years everyone told us what great parents we would be. But I was very afraid that if those same people could see inside our closed doors they would be very disappointed. Here's one thing I knew for sure ... I had done a lot of things in my life. But I had NEVER done anything as hard as being a Mom.

Being an adoptive Mom was an experience completely different than a bringing home a new baby from the hospital. When you give birth to a child you have nine months to bond with that child. As an adoptive parent you expect that bond to be as instantaneous as it is when you give birth. The truth, however, is that while you love that child immediately by choice, by a commitment you have made ... it sometimes takes a little more time to get down in your bones.

That's the situation I found myself in. I had made a promise, a commitment to love and nurture and take care of a strong-willed, funny, hot-headed, charming, loving, beautiful little girl. I had taken her into my home and made her part of my family. I loved her with the agape kind of love -- a love that is based on a commitment. But I didn't always like her. I struggled for that forever attachment that we needed as a family.

We were fortunate to have a good friend volunteer to provide daycare for Ella when I returned to work. Cassie had a real heart for our daughter and seemed to have a better handle on her moods than I did. I knew we would get there, and I felt terribly guilty about it, but for now I couldn't wait to return to work.

KARMEN BERNACCHI

15 - A COMPLICATED DIAGNOSIS

*"Look up at the sky and count the stars—
if indeed you can count them." Then He said to him,
"So shall your offspring be."*-- Genesis 15:5(NIV)

We knew that Ella was developmentally delayed. She didn't start to walk until almost 22 months old. She babbled, but had no real words. She was simply not meeting the expectations one would have of a "normal" child. And yet, her chromosome test was normal – so we clung to the fact that it must just be institution related delays, and prayed that in a loving family she would begin to thrive.

We still had the issue of her heart to deal with, so we made an appointment with a pediatric cardiologist to have a closer look at her heart. An echocardiogram confirmed that she indeed did have a hole in her heart – perhaps just a little larger than they anticipated, and a valve that was leaking just a bit. While they felt we would need to address the issues with surgery later on, they wanted to give her more time to grow first. She was so tiny, and she would handle the surgery much better if she were just a little bit bigger.

But the cardiologist was troubled by other anomalies she detected, particularly a skin tag that she had near her left ear. She said that was usually a sign of a genetic issue. She suggested we see a geneticist who could perhaps give us more insight into Ella's health and background.

We made the appointment anxious to see if she could help us gain better insight and ideas, but were distraught when the first words out of her mouth were, "Oh, she has Down syndrome."

"What? No! We waited weeks for the tests to come back. And the tests were clear. Her chromosomes were normal."

"I'm sure they only did the basic test," she said. "If the tests came back normal then she must have Mosaic Down syndrome. But she has all the classic signs," she said as she began to point to all the things that she could see physically in our daughter that pointed to the chromosome abnormality.

As she went down the list of all the things that were "wrong" with my daughter, I began to cry. As tears dripped off my chin, the last 16 years played over in my mind like an old movie clip. The years of infertility. The failed adoptions. The long wait to adopt. How could God do this to me? After so much heartbreak, how could He ask me to take on a child that had such high special needs? It wasn't fair! I was devastated. I was angry. I was terrified.

The geneticist suggested we could get a full array chromosome test which would look deeper into the genetic makeup. But the cost was about $2,000 and it wouldn't be covered by insurance. She said it was up to us, but in her professional opinion the tests would only serve to confirm her diagnosis of Mosaic Down syndrome.

We had just spent all of our savings plus some going to China. We didn't have the $2,000 to spend, so we opted to forego the tests at least for the time being.

As we grappled with the diagnosis of Mosaic Down syndrome, we headed to our next specialist – the otolaryngologist, because one thing was clear. Ella was not hearing like she should be.

A quick look in her ears told the doctor that Ella had "glue ears." She had extremely narrow ear canals (another sign of a chromosome disorder) and fluid had gotten trapped in the middle ear creating a thick glue like substance that had reduced her hearing to the level of "hearing underwater." She would need surgery to correct it. We scheduled the surgery and were thrilled to notice a marked difference in her response post-surgery.

Still the diagnosis of Mosaic Down syndrome hung over my head. I tried to tell myself that it was just a label, and it wouldn't change anything. But I just had to know for sure. We couldn't afford it, but I needed to know. Was her diagnosis accurate? I called and scheduled the full array test.

About a week later we got the phone call. "Well, it isn't Down syndrome or Mosaic Down's."

My heart leapt for joy, "YES!" I thought to myself. "I told you!"

"BUT," he continued. "I'm afraid it might have been better for her if it were Down syndrome. Down syndrome children qualify for all sorts of programs. Unfortunately, this is a syndrome that not much is known about. Ella has 18q- deletion syndrome. She also has a trisomy 13 translocation which is why they hadn't seen it on her previous test. The duplicated chromosome was sitting where the 18th chromosome normally is."

"18q- deletion syndrome?" I asked. "I've never heard of such a thing."

"It is extremely rare," said the geneticist. "I have never seen a case myself, but it is marked with a variety of health concerns. There's really no blueprint of what you can expect. She could suffer from profound mental retardation or she could be almost normal. It depends greatly on the location of the deletion and what material is missing." The geneticist went on to tell me that 25% of people that have 18q- deletion syndrome suffer from psychotic disorders. Ella's future looked anything but "normal".

We were crushed. Again I found myself angry. Angry that God would allow us to go down this path that seemed so far beyond us. This was not my dream. This was not the life we planned for ourselves. And we had a choice. Hadn't we heard from God? Did we make the wrong decision? I was overwhelmed and overcome with fear.

Friends and family offered up thoughtful words, but kind as they were, they were spoken from people who lived "normal" lives. Their children were destined to be successful business professionals or doctors or teachers or lawyers or ministers. They couldn't feel my pain. How could they? They didn't live with the fear that their child might never learn to read; that they might never be able to hold a meaningful conversation with you; that they might never be self-sufficient.

As I struggled to find peace with the diagnosis, I happened across a story by Emily Perl Kingsley that somehow verbalized the pain I was feeling. It's called "Welcome to Holland" …

I am often asked to describe the experience of raising a child with a disability - to try to help people who have not shared that unique experience to understand it, to imagine how it would feel. It's like this……

When you're going to have a baby, it's like planning a fabulous vacation trip - to Italy. You buy a bunch of guide books and make your wonderful plans. The Coliseum. The Michelangelo David. The gondolas in Venice. You may learn some handy phrases in Italian. It's all very exciting.

After months of eager anticipation, the day finally arrives. You pack your bags and off you go. Several hours later, the plane lands. The flight attendant comes in and says, "Welcome to Holland."

"<u>Holland</u>?!?" you say. "What do you mean Holland?? I signed up for Italy! I'm supposed to be in Italy. All my life I've dreamed of going to Italy."

But there's been a change in the flight plan. They've landed in Holland and there you must stay.

The important thing is that they haven't taken you to a horrible, disgusting, filthy place, full of pestilence, famine and disease. It's just a different place.

So you must go out and buy new guide books. And you must learn a whole new language. And you will meet a whole new group of people you would never have met.

It's just a <u>different</u> place. It's slower-paced than Italy, less flashy than Italy. But after you've been there for a while and you catch your breath, you look around.... and you begin to notice that Holland has windmills....and Holland has tulips. Holland even has Rembrandts.

But everyone you know is busy coming and going from Italy... and they're all bragging about what a wonderful time they had there. And for the rest of your life, you will say "Yes, that's where I was supposed to go. That's what I had planned."

And the pain of that will never, ever, ever, ever go away... because the loss of that dream is a very very significant loss.

But... if you spend your life mourning the fact that you didn't get to Italy, you may never be free to enjoy the very special, the very lovely things ... about Holland.

It wasn't that I didn't like Holland. It's just that I had prayed and planned and pinned all my hopes and dreams on Italy. This detour scared me to death. And I truly didn't know if I had the energy and patience to travel through Holland.

As fear continued to grip my heart God reminded me of a conversation I'd had with Him several years earlier while we were still waiting to become parents. I was praying -- complaining really -- to God about how He promised Abraham his seed would outnumber the stars in the sky, and yet at this rate we'd be lucky if we even had one. And I heard God whisper to my heart, "Maybe not ... but the one I give you will be especially bright."

Especially bright? "NO! God you promised us our child would be 'especially bright'. How could this be?" For years I'd been counting on a child with above average intelligence. Here we were being told our daughter might never learn to speak. She might never learn to read. She might never be able to do the things other children do. So how was it possible that she would be 'especially bright'. Was my imagination just going into overdrive that day. At the time God's voice seemed so clear – now I just wasn't sure.

As my own grief engulfed me, I found myself thinking once again about the Bible story that had initiated that conversation with

God -- Abraham and Sarah. They knew the pain of infertility. They, too, had longed for a child. And so when God told Abraham that he would be a father of many nations it had to seem a little "off". He must have thought he'd heard wrong. How could it be?? They were old. Well past the age of child bearing. It seemed an impossibility ... but GOD ... God had a plan that was anything but average for their family. He had a plan for a miracle. Could it be that God had a plan for a miracle for our little girl too? Was that possible?

I determined to set my grief aside and to begin to speak God's promises over Ella's life. "God, You promised me a child that was 'especially bright'. I claim that promise and I pray that You will bring it to pass in her life." Each morning I would (and still do) pray it over her. I thanked God for the 'especially bright' little girl He had given us and prayed for the fulfillment of His promise.

Then something happened as I began to pray and speak these promises over Ella's life. God changed ME. I became less consumed with the milestones I felt she should be hitting. I worried less about comparisons to other children her age. I began to see her in the light that God saw her. A beautiful little girl with a personality that was second to none.

We don't know what 'especially bright' means. Initially I thought it meant above average intelligence. But the more we have gotten to know her, we realize it may instead be her personality that is the 'especially bright' side of Ella. Regardless, I am convinced that

God spoke those words to my heart long before Ella was even born, because He knew that I would need something to hold on to as we struggled with the diagnosis of 18q- deletion syndrome; as we sat with the geneticist who told us just how little our child would be able to do; as we looked at report cards and worried that our child would never make the grade.

God didn't create a defective little girl. He created an 'especially bright' little girl. Sometimes I joke that the gene that God left out was the "mean gene," because Ella is almost always happy. She loves people and has a real joyful spirit. Her chromosomes are different than other folks, because she is different than other folks. She is not like other children, but that doesn't mean she is less valuable. She is exactly who God created her to be. She is 'bright' ... 'especially bright' ... and no geneticist's report can alter the promises of God.

16 - A MATTER OF THE HEART

"He sent forth His word and healed them.
He rescued them from the grave." Psalm 107:20 (NIV)

Purple … it's a beautiful color, unless it is the color of your hands and feet. Purple is a color that we witnessed continually on Ella's hands and feet. The color alarmed us, because we knew it was a sign that her heart was simply not doing its job well.

Her cardiologist was concerned too, but she was more concerned that Ella put on more weight before we attempted a surgery. She was at 0% on the growth charts, and had made very little progress in her growth. It was kind of a vicious circle. She needed to grow so that her surgery would be a success. But she needed the surgery in order to grow. Finally, the doctors agreed. The surgery should not be delayed any longer.

We went into the day confident that the surgery would be a success. We knew there were risks, but we also knew that the surgery was critical to her long-term health and wellness. She was surrounded by loved ones as they wheeled her away to the operating room, and together we waited for a good report.

It wasn't very long into the surgery that her surgeon came out with an alarming report. They had discovered that the small hole they had seen on the echocardiogram was not so small after all. In fact, it was "very large". So large in fact that they didn't think that the largest plug they had would fit it. When Ella had her echocardiogram they did not recognize that Ella's heart was not sitting in her body correctly. It was turned sideways. This made getting a clear look at the hole impossible.

The heart was turned sideways because she had a lung that did not develop in utero ... it was very small and had undeveloped blood vessels and no capillaries going to it. It was essentially non-functioning. When the surgeon told us it was a shock to us. She has had several bouts of pneumonia, but we had no idea there were other issues to worry about.

He was honest and told us that he really didn't know what to do about the lung. It was very unusual and neither he nor the pulmonary team had ever seen anything like it. He said they would want to take a month to study it and confer with other specialists across the U.S. to see if they could come up with a solution.

In the meantime, he asked us what we wanted to do about her heart surgery. He wasn't confident that they would be able to make the plug work, but they could try. We told him to proceed. Her heart needed to be fixed, and by fixing the hole it would take pressure off her good lung which was functioning at 240% of a healthy person's lung. The doctor told us if her heart wasn't fixed that her good lung would eventually wear out from being overtaxed.

As the surgical team moved forward with surgery, we took to social media requesting prayer for our daughter. We needed a miracle. Greg joined our family for lunch in the hospital cafeteria, but I couldn't leave the waiting room. I just felt the overwhelming need to stay as close as possible to my daughter. While they were gone, the surgeon came out with an excellent report. The surgery was a success. The doctor was elated and so was I. But in all honesty, we were not really surprised ... we had been praying, and we felt confident that God had her heart in His hands. After a day of recovery they sent us home ... and Ella was bouncing off the walls again in literally hours.

The lung was another story ... we waited a month and went back to the UW-Madison Children's Hospital for a CT scan. It was a Friday and by the time Ella's procedure was complete, the doctors had already gone home for the day, so we had to wait for a call with results.

The phone call finally came, and we rejoiced when we heard the doctor tell us "I have been struggling to come up with an explanation for what we see ... but truly it is a mystery." You see, Ella's lung had grown and it had new capillaries going to it and it was now functioning NORMALLY!

"How can this be?" I asked the doctor. "Is this something that happened because her heart was fixed?"

"No," said the doctor. "That is not something that we would expect from her heart surgery. To be honest it is just one of those things that we simply cannot find an answer for." The only thing he could really tell me was that it was no longer an issue and that our daughter was truly a lucky little girl.

We know this was no "mystery" and we also knew our little girl was not simply "lucky". We had been blessed with a MIRACLE. God has had His hand on our little girl from day one, and despite the many challenges she has faced, He showed us that day more than ever before that HE is taking care of her and we could trust Him.

17 - STILL WAITING

"But as for me, I watch in hope
for the LORD, *I wait for God my Savior;*
my God will hear me. – Micah 7:7(NIV)

Life with a special needs daughter is not always easy. Ella is an amazing little girl. She is caring. She is funny. She is happy and full of life. She is also unstoppable. These are all great traits. But sometimes the full of life and unstoppable aspects of her are simply more than our middle age bodies are equipped to handle.

Her high energy and our middle agedness presents challenges of its own. We don't have the same support systems that younger parents do. Younger parents can leave their kids with Grandma and Grandpa. Ella's grandparents, however, are at an age where it is impossible to keep up with her.

Younger parents have friends with kids and they take turns babysitting for each other. Because of our age, we have never fit into those social circles, so find ourselves feeling "on our own" for the most part. And when you're dealing with an unstoppable force like Ella, that leaves her middle age parents feeling tired – VERY tired most of the time. We are fortunate to have a few close friends and family members that have stepped up for us when we have really needed a break, and they have helped us avoid nervous breakdowns.

Ella's energy is a constant struggle wherever we go. Her teachers send us notes at least a couple times a week. "Ella would not sit still during class." "Ella ran out of the classroom today." "Ella will not stay in her space at lunch. She is always getting up and running around or getting in other children's faces." "We are concerned that Ella's inability to focus is keeping her from learning."

Ella does great when the setting is all about playtime, but taking her anywhere where she needs to sit still finds us feeling overwhelmed with frustration. Getting Ella to sit still is like trying to settle a bucking bronco. She just has to be moving.

I have left church in tears more than a few times as I have struggled to keep our daughter still, while she has sapped me of every ounce of energy I had. Rather than leaving feeling recharged for the week ahead, I have left feeling completely drained and helpless.

I close out almost every day by telling God how incapable I am of raising our little girl. I'm not strong enough or smart enough. I don't have the energy required. I am tired. I am old. I'm weak. I don't have what it takes ... and yet he closes out my day with the words from Isaiah 40:29-31 (KJV): *"He giveth power to the faint; and to them that have no might he increaseth strength. Even the youths shall faint and be weary, and the young men shall utterly fall: But they that wait upon the* L*ORD shall renew their strength; they shall mount up with wings as eagles; they shall run, and not be weary; and they shall walk, and not faint."*

And there is that word again – "WAIT".

Before we adopted Ella, "wait" was an ugly four-letter word. I spent years questioning whether God heard me or cared for me or even knew I existed. But during that wait for our daughter, I learned to trust Him. I learned that He is faithful.

Today we wait as God unveils the "especially bright" little girl that He has promised our daughter would be. Some days I cry out of pure exhaustion, "God I hope you know what you're doing!" Some days I feel like giving up. But then He reminds me of the miracles He has already performed in our daughter's life. And I know that He is not through with her yet.

A few months ago I got a different kind of call -- "cancer". While the weight of that word struck fear in me at first, I would come to almost appreciate it in the months ahead. As our journey to adopt helped me trust in the promises of God; so my journey through cancer has helped me embrace just how precious life is.

I was fortunate. They caught it early. My cancer story was short, and the prognosis is excellent. And yet it was a reminder to me that tomorrow is not promised to anyone. We can spend our lives longing for something else ahead, or we can hold on to each moment and savor the time we have been given.

I'm still waiting. But I am learning that waiting time does not have to be wasting time. I believe it is in the waiting times that God teaches us the most beautiful lessons of life.

God came to Abraham when he was seventy-five and told him he was going to be a father, the ancestor of a great nation. How long was it before that promise was fulfilled? Twenty-four years. Abraham had to wait.

God told the Israelites that they would leave their slavery in Egypt and become a nation. But the people had to wait four hundred years.

God told Moses he would lead the people to the Promised Land. But they had to wait forty years in the wilderness.

In the Bible, waiting is so closely associated with faith that sometimes the two words are used interchangeably. The great promise of the Old Testament was that a Messiah would come. But Israel had to wait — generation after generation, century after century.

But even the arrival of Jesus did not mean that the waiting was over. Jesus lived, taught, was crucified, was resurrected, and was about to ascend into heaven when His friends asked Him, "Lord, will you restore the kingdom now?" That is, "Can we stop waiting?" And

Jesus had one more command: *"Do not leave Jerusalem, but wait for the gift my Father promised."*

And the Holy Spirit came — but that still did not mean that the time of waiting was over. Paul wrote in Romans 8:23-25 (KJV), *"We ourselves, who have the first fruits of the Spirit, groan inwardly while we wait for adoption to sonship, the redemption of our bodies. For in hope we were saved. Now hope that is seen is not hope. For who hopes for what is seen? But if we hope for what we do not see, we wait for it with patience."*

Forty-three times in the Old Testament alone, the people are commanded, *"Wait. Wait on the Lord."* Waiting is part of God's plan. It's in the waiting times that He makes us who He wants us to be.

Today I look back at all God's brought me through. I look ahead to His promises, and I can rest, knowing that the God who made Abraham the father of many nations was the same God who heard this broken woman's cry for a child. He is the same God who protected an 8 month old baby girl left alone, abandoned on a busy roadside in Pingdingshan, Henan, China. And He is the same God that holds our lives in the palm of His hand.

In the words of David, may I forever remember where to keep my trust. *"Let the morning bring me word of Your unfailing love, for I have put my trust in You. Show me the way I should go, for to you I entrust my life." Psalm 143:8 (NIV)*

KARMEN BERNACCHI

PHOTO ALBUM

The early days ... my brothers Kevin, Kent and I at the Assembly of God church my father pastored in Elroy, Wisconsin. This was just one of the many places we lived in my younger days.

I married the love of my life, Greg Bernacchi, on October 7, 1995 – and thus our journey began. *(Me and my Dad pictured below.)*

One of the highlights of our waiting time was a ministry trip to Alaska.

WAITING FOR A FAMILY

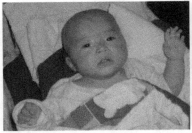 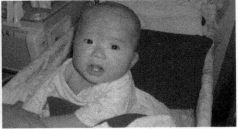

The above photos are the earliest known photos of Ella, taken in the hospital in Pingdingshan, Henan, China the day she was found.

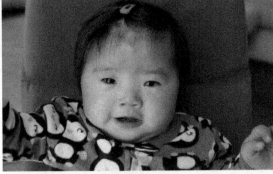

Ella's referral photos. These were the first photos we saw of our beautiful daughter. We fell in love instantly.

BEING LOVED AT MORNING STAR FAMILY HOME

It was an answer to prayer that Ella was placed at Morning Star Family Home in Beijing. They prayed for her, cared for her and loved her like their own.

OUR "GOTCHA" MOMENT

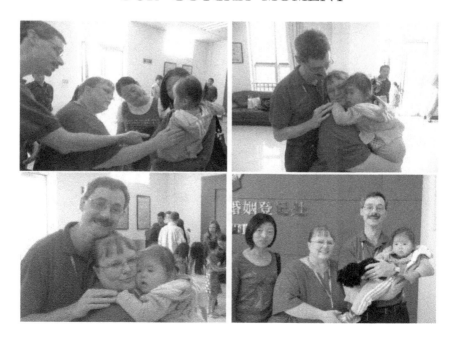

THE NEW FAMILY IN CHINA

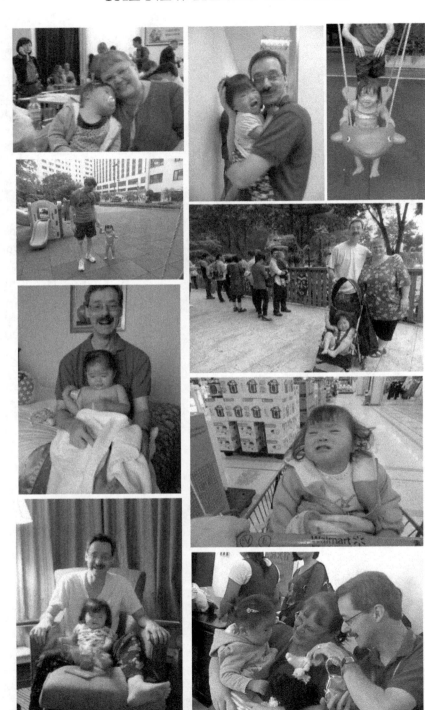

FINALLY HOME!

Finally home. There were very few photos taken in those early days that didn't include a bucket on her head.

A FEW FAMILY MEMORIES

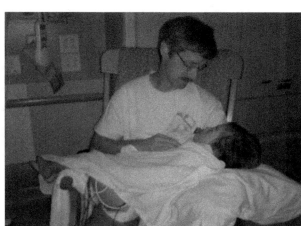
Greg and Ella after her miracle heart surgery.

Ella's cousins quickly became her best friends.

Gardening with Aunt Sue.

Ella will dress up like a princess if you really want her to ... but what she really wants to be is a robot!

ACKNOWLEDGMENTS

As I think about our journey there are so many people that deserve my gratitude. First and foremost, I wish to thank my heavenly Father. I cannot imagine trying to go through life without You. Thank You for the many blessings You have bestowed on me. Thank You also for never giving up on me!

Next, to my amazing husband and best friend. Greg, you have supported every dream I have ever had. You have held me through the tough times and rejoiced with me in the good. You are the best person I have ever known, and I am so grateful for the love we share. I adore you!

To my Mom, I have learned so much from you as you have gone through tough times. Your steadfast faith has inspired me and encouraged me. Thank you for the many prayers and for giving me courage to hold on in the tough times!

To Mom Bernacchi, it was your inheritance that allowed us to start this journey. I wish that you could have met your granddaughter. She would have loved you so much. Thank you for your gift – I look forward to seeing you and Dad Bernacchi again someday in heaven!

To the "Bersnodson's", thank you for loving Ella so much. You guys may be the only ones that never gave up on us bringing Ella home. And since she has been home you have loved her so unconditionally. We think of you as our kids too – we are so blessed by this little family within a family. We love you guys!

To my brother Kevin, you have been such a great friend and support in our ministry and our lives. Through our "waiting" years you listened to our hearts and shared in our dream. You are always there to lend a hand and such a blessing to our family. Thank you!

To those that gave us financial support for our journey – KJ & Donna, Joy & Richie, Paul & Janay, Kent & Sarah -- we can never thank you enough for all that you did. You helped make our dream come true – and you helped ensure a sweet orphan girl had the chance for a future. Thank you!

To those that have given us respite when we needed a break, we are so very grateful for your support. Cassie, Faith & Nick, Katie & Josh, Jamie & Gina, Mark & Sarah, Paul & Janay, Terry & Nicole, Tom & Mary Jane, Jess & Ken, the Bolton family – truly we would be lost without you. There have been so many times when we have just needed a night out or some time to stop and sleep (if the truth be told!) You have been there for us and we are so very grateful!

To Tom & Sue, thank you for being there for us on that long journey home and so many times since. I don't know what we would have done without you. And Sue, your advice and wisdom for helping Ella achieve has been such a blessing to us. I appreciate you more than you will ever know!

To Pastor Paul, Doreen and the people of Faith Christian Church -- thank you for your encouraging words and prayers. We have worked together, prayed together and walked out our faith together … you have been a blessing to us in so many ways. We are honored to serve with you!

To Kurt & Seleena, thank you for lending us your kids when we needed a "kid fix". There were so many times on our long journey to parenthood that I just needed the love of a child to help me hold on. Your children have always been very special to me.

To Jamie & Gina, thanks for being the best Godparents in the world. Ella loves you so much and we are so grateful for the love and support you show us and our little girl. You are such a blessing!

To Grandma (Anna Anderson) and Melodee & Richard. I know I can always count on your prayers and words of wisdom when the road gets tough. I treasure you and am so grateful for your love!

To our friends and family members that prayed for us and encouraged us along the way. While it is impossible to mention everyone by name, we want you to know that each kind word, each thought, each word of encouragement have meant more than you will ever know and will forever be remembered.

Finally, to the Ladybugs, I never dreamed I would make such amazing friends when I joined that China Adoption Yahoo! group so many years ago. We prayed for each other, cried with each other, rejoiced with each other and supported each other on this long difficult journey. Today I still consider you my among my closest friends. You will forever be my adoption family!

ABOUT THE AUTHOR

Karmen Bernacchi grew up in a Christian home and was adopted into God's family at just three years old. From a young age she has remained active in her church and serving through ministry. She attended Evangel College after high school and lived in Minneapolis for a few years before settling in central Wisconsin.

She met her husband Greg while performing in community theatre. Shortly after their marriage, the couple formed Karmen & Greg Ministries – a music and drama ministry dedicated to using comedy, drama and song to reach across denominational lines.

After 16 years of fertility treatments and failed adoption attempts, Karmen and her husband Greg traveled to China in the fall of 2011 to bring home their daughter Ella Joy SiHan. Ella was born with a serious heart and lung defect and 18q- deletion syndrome. Though their journey as a family has been challenging at times, God has used it to deepen their faith and dependence on Him.

If you are interested in having Karmen & Greg minister with your church or group, please email kgbernacchi@gmail.com.